Tony Romo

by Kathy Allen

Consultant: Barry Wilner
AP Football Writer

BEARPORT
PUBLISHING

New York, New York

Credits
Cover and Title Page, © James D Smith/AP Images and G. Newman Lowrence/AP Images; 4, © Mike McCarn/AP Images; 5, © Paul Spinelli/AP Images; 6, © Ronald Martinez/ Getty Images; 7, © Chuck Burton/AP Images; 8, © David J. Phillip/AP Images; 9, © The Journal-Times; 10, © Allen Fredrickson/Icon SMI; 11, © David Stluka/AP Images; 12, © Seth Poppel/Yearbook Library; 13, © The Journal-Times; 14, © Eastern Illinois/Collegiate Images/ Getty Images; 15, © Alan Look/Icon SMI; 16, © Thomas B. Shea/Icon SMI; 17, © Donna McWilliam/AP Images; 18, © Matt Slocum/AP Images; 19, © David J. Phillip/AP Images; 20, © Bill Nichols/AP Images; 21, © Henry Ray Abrams/AP Images; 22, © Paul Spinelli/AP Images.

Publisher: Kenn Goin
Editorial Director: Adam Siegel
Creative Director: Spencer Brinker
Photo Researcher: Arnold Ringstad
Design: Emily Love

Library of Congress Cataloging-in-Publication Data
Allen, Kathy.
  Tony Romo / by Kathy Allen.
      p. cm. — (Football stars up close)
  Includes bibliographical references and index.
  ISBN 978-1-61772-719-1 (library binding) — ISBN 1-61772-719-9 (library binding)
 1. Romo, Tony, 1980—Juvenile literature. 2. Football players—United States—Biography— Juvenile literature. 3. Quarterbacks (Football)—United States—Biography—Juvenile literature. I. Title.
  GV939.R646A45 2013
  796.332092—dc23
  [B]
                                     2012038165

For more information, write to Bearport Publishing Company, Inc., 45 West 21st Street, Suite 3B, New York, New York 10010. Printed in the United States of America.

10 9 8 7 6 5 4 3 2 1

Contents

Backup No More 4

Tony's Touchdown 6

Sports Standout 8

An Early Football Fan 10

High School Starter 12

Playing in Illinois 14

Tony the Pro 16

An NFL Star 18

Staying Strong 20

Tony's Life and Career 22

Glossary 23

Index 24

Bibliography 24

Read More 24

Learn More Online 24

Backup No More

Tony Romo joined the Dallas Cowboys as a **quarterback** in 2003. However, he spent most of his time on the bench as a **backup**. That changed in the 2006 season. The Cowboys' starting quarterback, Drew Bledsoe, was throwing fewer **touchdowns** than before. The team's coach decided to give Tony a chance to play. It was near the end of a game against the Houston Texans. Would Tony be able to score a touchdown?

Tony (right) speaks with his coach before a 2006 game.

Tony throws a ball during practice in 2006.

A starter is any player who is the coach's first choice to play in a game.

Tony's Touchdown

Fans cheered from the stands as Tony ran onto the field. The Cowboys and the Texans lined up, and the play began. Tony wanted to score—and fast. He quickly passed the ball to move his team down the field. Then, he threw the ball to his teammate Terrell Owens in the **end zone**. The ball shot through the air right into Terrell's arms! It was Tony Romo's first touchdown pass in the **NFL**. The Cowboys won the game 34–6. Tony was ready to be a starting quarterback!

Tony throws the touchdown pass to Terrell Owens.

Tony (right) with
Terrell Owens (left)

The Dallas Cowboys play
in Texas. **Home games** are played
at Cowboys Stadium. The stadium
was built in 2009 at a cost
of one billion dollars.

Sports Standout

Anthony "Tony" Romo was born on April 21, 1980, in San Diego, California. His family moved to Burlington, Wisconsin, when he was two years old. Surprisingly, Tony didn't play a lot of football as a child. He did, however, love sports. He played basketball, baseball, and golf.

When Tony was eight years old, he got his first set of golf clubs for Christmas. He went outside to try them out. On his first swing, he hit the ball right into his neighbor's window—and broke it.

Tony still enjoys playing golf today.

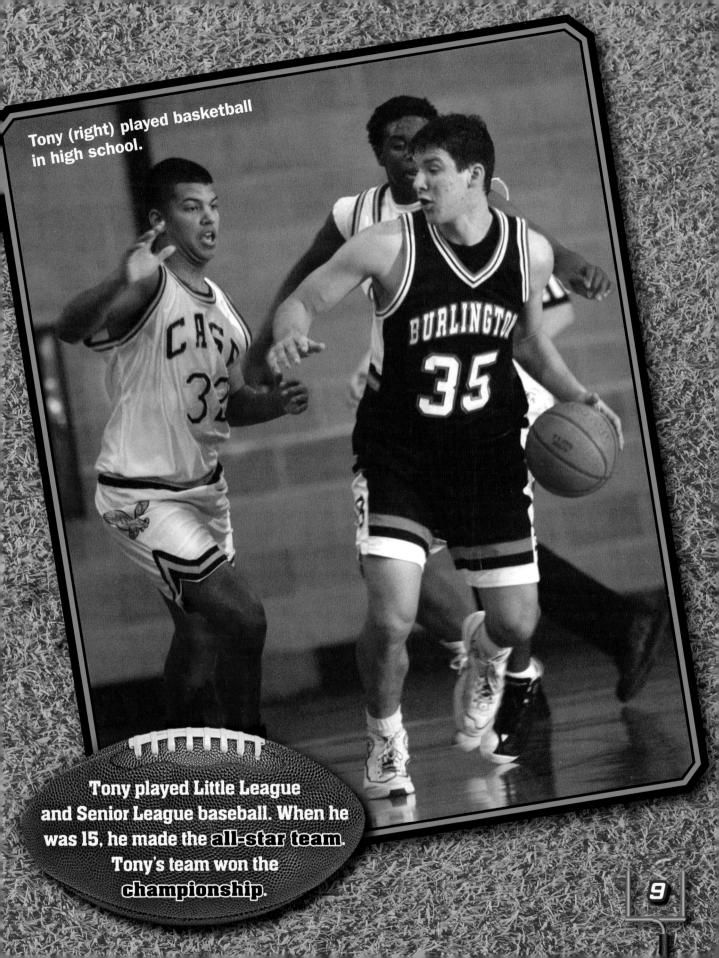

Tony (right) played basketball in high school.

Tony played Little League and Senior League baseball. When he was 15, he made the **all-star team**. Tony's team won the **championship**.

An Early Football Fan

Tony didn't join a football team as a child. However, he still loved to watch the games. Because Wisconsin is home to the Green Bay Packers, the Packers became Tony's favorite NFL team. He especially loved to watch their quarterback Brett Favre throw touchdown passes.

As a child, Tony was a fan of Packers quarterback Brett Favre.

Brett Favre holds the record for starting the most games as a quarterback. Between 1992 and 2010, he started 297 straight games.

Brett Favre is known for his powerful passes.

High School Starter

At Burlington High School in Wisconsin, Tony wanted to play soccer. However, the school didn't have enough players for a team. So he tried out for football instead.

Tony impressed his high school coach and made the team. Thanks to his strong arm and powerful passes, Tony became the starting quarterback by his third year. During his third and fourth years, he became a star player. He led his team to two big wins in the **playoffs**.

Tony's yearbook photo from his senior year

Tony became a star player
in high school.

Tony graduated from
Burlington High School in 1998.
In his senior year, he was
named the best athlete
in his class.

13

Playing in Illinois

Tony went to Eastern Illinois University in 1998. There, he was no longer the star player. In his first year, he was not even a starting player. The other players were bigger, stronger, and tougher. Tony kept practicing, however, and in his second year he became starting quarterback. His hard work to be a better player paid off. He led his team to the playoffs three years in a row!

Tony throws the ball while playing for the Eastern Illinois University Panthers.

Tony avoids a tackle during a college game.

Tony won the Walter Payton Award in his senior year. This award is given to an outstanding college football player.

Tony the Pro

Tony set his sights on playing in the NFL. Still, he would need to prove himself yet again. Tony was not chosen by any team in the 2003 **draft**. None of them thought he was good enough to become a star quarterback. Soon after the draft, however, the Dallas Cowboys signed him as a backup player. Unfortunately, Tony rarely got a chance to show off his skills on the field.

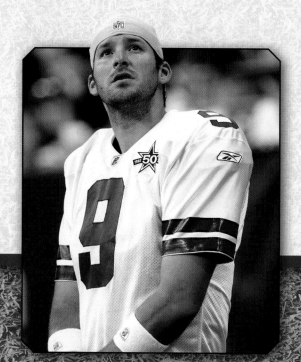

Tony watches a game from the sidelines.

Tony (center) practices with other Cowboys quarterbacks in 2003.

Professional football teams choose new players each year in the NFL draft. The draft has been held every year since 1936.

An NFL Star

Tony played as a backup for the Cowboys for three years. His touchdown against the Texans in 2006, however, proved he was ready for something greater. Two weeks later, Tony became the Dallas Cowboys' starting quarterback. His powerful arm and **accurate** passing helped him lead the Cowboys to the playoffs that year. Amazingly, in 2007, Tony led his team to the playoffs once again. Tony had become one of the NFL's top quarterbacks. Fans were thrilled—and so was Tony.

Tony calls a play during a 2006 game against the Detroit Lions.

Tony runs with the ball during a 2007 playoff game against the New York Giants.

Tony was picked for the **NFL Pro Bowl**, the NFL's all-star game, after the 2006, 2007, and 2009 seasons.

Staying Strong

Tony and the Cowboys seemed unstoppable. He led the team to the playoffs again in 2009. Tony tried to bring the Cowboys to the playoffs once more in 2010. Unfortunately, Tony hurt his collarbone during a game in October. As a result, he missed most of the season. Luckily, his collarbone healed in time for Tony to play every game in 2011. With lots of hard work, Tony has earned his position as a star in the NFL.

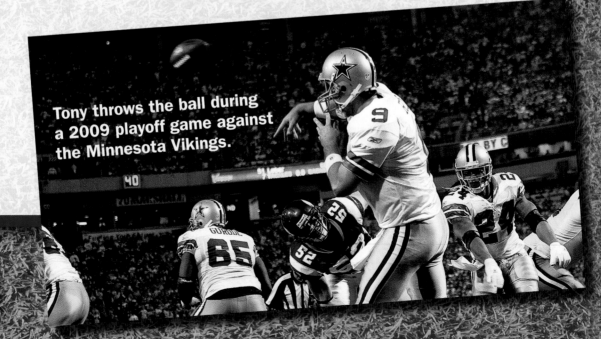

Tony throws the ball during a 2009 playoff game against the Minnesota Vikings.

Tony celebrates during a 2011 game against the New York Jets.

Tony visits young players at his football camp in Wisconsin each year. He tells them to work hard, saying, "You don't know where you can be one or two years from now."

Tony's Life and Career

★ **April 21, 1980** Anthony "Tony" Romo is born in San Diego, California.

★ **1982** Tony's family moves to Burlington, Wisconsin.

★ **1995** Tony's Little League team wins a championship.

★ **1998** Tony goes to college at Eastern Illinois University in Charleston, Illinois.

★ **2003** The Dallas Cowboys sign Tony to play on their team as a backup.

★ **2006** Tony makes his first start as an NFL quarterback. He leads the Cowboys to the playoffs.

★ **2007** Tony leads the Cowboys to the playoffs a second time.

★ **2009** The Cowboys go to the playoffs again but lose to the Minnesota Vikings.

★ **2010** Tony's season is cut short by a broken collarbone.

★ **2011** Tony plays every game, throwing 31 touchdowns in the season.

Glossary

accurate (AK-yuh-ruht)
on target; free from mistakes

all-star team (AWL-star TEEM)
a team made up of the best players in an area

backup (BAK-uhp)
a player who does not start playing at the beginning of a game and often does not play at all

championship (CHAM-pee-uhn-s*hip*)
a contest or final game of a series that decides which team will be the winner

draft (DRAFT)
an event in which NFL teams take turns choosing college players to play for them

end zone (END ZOHN)
the area at either end of a football field where touchdowns are scored

home games (HOHM GAYMZ)
games that a team plays in its own stadium

NFL (EN-EFF-ELL)
letters standing for the National Football League, which includes 32 teams

playoffs (PLAY-awfss)
the games held after the end of the regular football season that determine which two teams will compete in the championship game

Pro Bowl (PRO BOHL)
the NFL's all-star game that is for the season's best NFL players

quarterback (KWOR-tur-bak)
a football player who leads the offense, the part of a team that moves the ball forward

touchdowns (TUHCH-*douns*)
scores of six points, made by getting the ball across the other team's goal line

Index

baseball 8–9
basketball 8–9
Bledsoe, Drew 4
Burlington High
    School 12–13
childhood 8–9, 10,
    12–13
Dallas Cowboys 4,
    6–7, 16–17, 18,
    20

Eastern Illinois
    University 14–15
Favre, Brett 10–11
golf 8
Green Bay Packers 10
high school 12–13
Houston Texans 4, 6,
    18

NFL draft 16–17
Owens, Terrell 6
playoffs 12, 14, 18–19,
    20
Wisconsin 8, 10, 12,
    21

Bibliography

Engel, Mac. *Tony Romo: America's Next Quarterback*. Chicago:
    Triumph Books (2007).

Official Web Site of the Dallas Cowboys: www.dallascowboys.com

Tony Romo's Official Web Site: www.tonyromo9.com

Read More

Sandler, Michael. *Tony Romo (Football Heroes Making a Difference)*.
    New York: Bearport (2010).

Savage, Jeff. *Tony Romo (Amazing Athletes)*. Minneapolis, MN:
    Lerner (2011).

Williams, Zella. *Tony Romo: Star Quarterback (Hispanic Headliners)*.
    New York: Rosen (2011).

Learn More Online

To learn more about Tony Romo, visit
www.bearportpublishing.com/FootballStarsUpClose